FARTY PANTS

A SOUND BOOK OF STINK

ERIC GERON

Illustrated by Alejandro O'Kif

becker&mayer! kids

FARTY PANTS

Push the 🔊 on each page to hear the sounds!

Play the music of the fart!

Is your tune a long, drawn-out sigh, a crackling wet pop, a string of putt-putt-putts, or a silent-but-stinky whoosh that only dogs can hear? Farting is completely natural, and extremely FUN! Especially in the comfort of your own home.

(Though you may not want Mama and Papa breaking wind in your face. That would really stink!)

Farts are digested gas leaving the body. They are made up of a mixture of things: nitrogen, hydrogen, carbon dioxide, methane, oxygen . . . and hydrogen sulfide, which is the smelly secret.

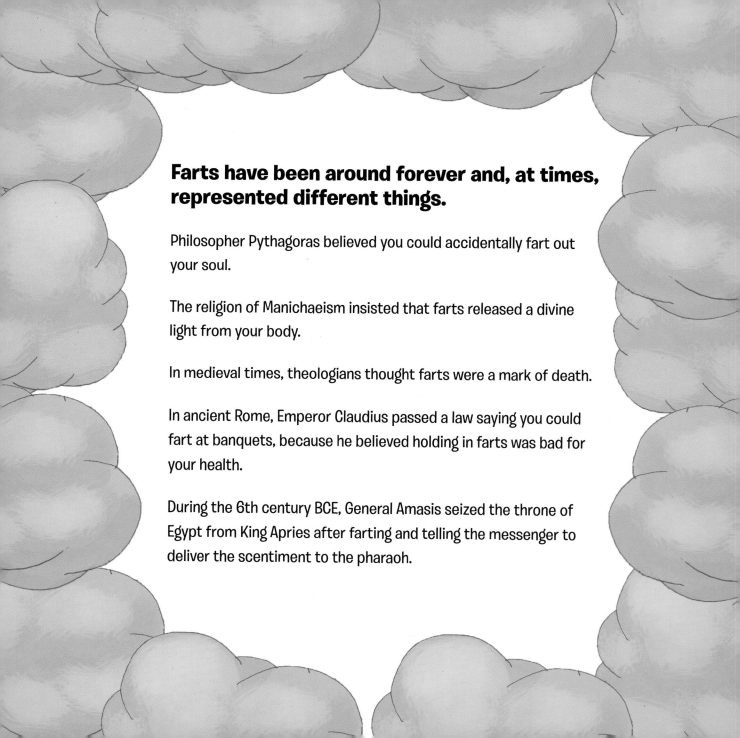

Farts have been around forever and, at times, represented different things.

Philosopher Pythagoras believed you could accidentally fart out your soul.

The religion of Manichaeism insisted that farts released a divine light from your body.

In medieval times, theologians thought farts were a mark of death.

In ancient Rome, Emperor Claudius passed a law saying you could fart at banquets, because he believed holding in farts was bad for your health.

During the 6th century BCE, General Amasis seized the throne of Egypt from King Apries after farting and telling the messenger to deliver the scentiment to the pharaoh.

No matter your beliefs, farts will always be a global fart-nomenon!

You may think that babies fart more than old people.

Babies are just learning to digest food, and they swallow big gulps of air whenever they cry or eat, creating a diaper full of farts.

You may think that old people fart more than babies.

Old people's digestive systems slow down as they age and being backed up can make them more gassy.

An old person's fart probably smells worse than a baby's fart, since poop stays in the colon longer when you're older. Just ask poor Granny Rhinoceros!

Play your trouser trumpet loud and proud!

A loud fart isn't always a smelly one. It probably means you have an upset tummy. But sometimes, if you're suffering from an upset stomach because of too much tuna, like Mr. Cool Cat, your fart can be loud and stinky.

THE LONGEST VERIFIED FART WAS BY BERNARD CLEMMENS OF LONDON: **2 MINUTES** AND **42 SECONDS!**

Three strikes and it's out . . . in the open.

The process of your fart spreading out to fill the air is called diffusion. Calculating the speed of a fart can be difficult due to many variables—like temperature and pressure.

Have you ever toot-tooted in your tutu before a captive audience?

It happens to all of us–even to historical figures and seemingly flawless (and fart-less) celebrities. Le Pétomane, French for Crazy Farts, was the stage name for Joseph Pujol, an entertainer born in 1857 who blew out candles and played the flute by . . . farting. Please, hold your applause.

DISNEY'S FIRST CHARACTER TO FART ON-SCREEN WAS **PUMBA** IN *THE LION KING.*

Have you ever farted in a pool or pond? Did you notice that the fart smelled worse underwater?

If you're taking a bath, your bathroom is probably humid.

The water vapor causes smells to remain in the air longer.

Astronauts fart in space!

But not for jet power or rocket propulsion. Astronaut suits have filters to remove gases.

People fart more when flying in airplanes or space shuttles due to the change in atmospheric pressure.

ASTRONAUT **JOHN YOUNG** WAS THE FIRST MAN TO FART ON THE MOON.

Have you ever realized that you enjoy the smell of your own farts?

That's completely normal! Your farts are a familiar smell thanks to your own unique stomach bacteria, even if they aren't quite as nice as unicorn farts are rumored to be.

And while most farts aren't heaven-scent or fartastical, the facts in this book may linger with you long, long after—like the best farts.

Quarto Knows

Brimming with creative inspiration, how-to projects, and useful information to enrich your everyday life, Quarto Knows is a favorite destination for those pursuing their interests and passions. Visit our site and dig deeper with our books into your area of interest: Quarto Creates, Quarto Cooks, Quarto Homes, Quarto Lives, Quarto Drives, Quarto Explores, Quarto Gifts, or Quarto Kids.

© 2021 Quarto Publishing Group USA Inc.

Published in 2021 by becker&mayer! kids, an imprint of The Quarto Group, 11120 NE 33rd Place, Suite 201, Bellevue, WA 98004 USA.

www.QuartoKnows.com

becker&mayer! kids titles are also available at discount for retail, wholesale, promotional, and bulk purchase. For details, contact the Special Sales Manager by email at specialsales@quarto.com or by mail at The Quarto Group, Attn: Special Sales Manager, 100 Cummings Center Suite 265D, Beverly, MA 01915 USA.

21 22 23 24 25   5 4 3 2 1

ISBN: 978-0-7603-6911-1

Library of Congress Cataloging-in-Publication Data available upon request.

Author: Eric Geron
Illustrator: Alejandro O'Kif
Illustrations © 2017 Quarto Publishing Group USA Inc. First published as Everyone Toots (ISBN: 978-1-63322-224-3) by MoonDance Press, an imprint of The Quarto Group.

Printed, manufactured, and assembled in Shenzhen, China, 12/20

MIX
Paper from responsible sources
FSC® C017606
www.fsc.org

#338546

INSTRUCTIONS FOR BATTERY REPLACEMENT:

The audio module includes three AG13 batteries (3x1.5V=4.5V). If the audio does not play, you may need to replace the batteries. Batteries should be replaced by adults only. Batteries are small and could possibly be ingested, so a child should never use this product unless the battery compartment has been properly secured. To replace the batteries, loosen the screw on top of the module and remove the battery door.

Remove the exhausted batteries and install new batteries using the correct polarity displayed on the battery door. Only use batteries of the same or equivalent type AG13.

Do not mix old and new batteries. Do not mix alkaline, standard (carbon-zinc), or rechargeable (nickel-cadmium) batteries. Do not use rechargeable batteries or attempt to recharge non-rechargeable batteries. Do not short circuit the supply terminals.

This product contains button batteries. If swallowed, a button battery could cause severe injury or death in just 2 hours. Seek medical attention immediately.

Note: This equipment has been tested and found to comply with the limits for a Class B digital device, pursuant to part 15 of the FCC Rules. These limits are designed to provide reasonable protection against harmful interference in a residential installation. This equipment generates, uses, and can radiate radio frequency energy and, if not installed and used in accordance with the instructions, may cause harmful interference to radio communications. However, there is no guarantee that interference will not occur in a particular installation. If this equipment does cause harmful interference to radio or television reception, which can be determined by turning the equipment off and on, the user is encouraged to try to correct the interference by one or more of the following measures:

- Reorient or relocate the receiving antenna.
- Increase the separation between the equipment and receiver.
- Connect the equipment into an outlet on a circuit different from that to which the receiver is connected.
- Consult the dealer or an experienced radio/TV technician for help.

This device complies with part 15 of the FCC Rules. Operation is subject to the following two conditions: (1) This device may not cause harmful interference, and (2) this device must accept any interference received, including interference that may cause undesired operation.

Note: Changes or modifications not expressly approved by the party responsible for compliance could void the user's authority to operate the equipment.

This Class B digital apparatus complies with Canadian ICE-003.